DOUGLAS
MACARTHUR
AMERICA'S GENERAL

SPECIAL LIVES IN HISTORY THAT BECOME

Signature LIVES

DOUGLAS
MACARTHUR
AMERICA'S GENERAL

by Brenda Haugen

Content Adviser: Major Bryan Gibby, Assistant Professor,
Department of History,
United States Military Academy, West Point, New York

Reading Adviser: Rosemary G. Palmer, Ph.D.,
Department of Literacy, College of Education,
Boise State University

COMPASS POINT BOOKS MINNEAPOLIS, MINNESOTA

Compass Point Books
3109 West 50th Street, #115
Minneapolis, MN 55410

Visit Compass Point Books on the Internet at *www.compasspointbooks.com*
or e-mail your request to *custserv@compasspointbooks.com*

Editor: Julie Gassman
Lead Designer: Jaime Martens
Page Production: The Design Lab
Photo Researchers: Jo Miller and Svetlana Zhurkin
Cartographer: XNR Productions, Inc.
Educational Consultant: Diane Smolinski

Managing Editor: Catherine Neitge
Creative Director: Keith Griffin
Editorial Director: Carol Jones

To Angie, Karen, Bernice, and Gerald. Your support and encouragement
mean more than you could ever know! BLH

Library of Congress Cataloging-in-Publication Data
Haugen, Brenda.
  Douglas MacArthur: America's General / by Brenda Haugen.
    p. cm. — (Signature lives)
  Includes bibliographical references and index.
  ISBN 0-7565-0994-7 (hard cover)
  1. MacArthur, Douglas, 1880–1964—Juvenile literature. 2. Generals—
United States—Biography—Juvenile literature. 3. United States. Army—
Biography—Juvenile literature. 4. United States—History, Military—20th
century—Juvenile literature. I. Title. II. Series.
  E745.M3H325 2006
  355'.0092—dc22   2005008823

MODERN AMERICA

Starting in the late 19th century, advancements in all areas of human activity transformed an old world into a new and modern place. Inventions prompted rapid shifts in lifestyle, and scientific discoveries began to alter the way humanity viewed itself. Beginning with World War I, warfare took place on a global scale, and ideas such as nationalism and communism showed that countries were taking a larger view of their place in the world. The combination of all these changes continues to produce what we know as the modern world.

Table of Contents

Chapter

1 A Tough Decision

❧⦿❧

Young Douglas MacArthur felt as if he was going to throw up. With his stomach churning, he sat in front of a court of officers at the U.S. Military Academy at West Point, New York. But from the looks of him on that December day in 1900, the officers would never have known that Douglas' nerves were on edge. At age 20, he had already learned to control his anxiety and present himself as a calm, confident cadet. Managing his emotions was a skill that would serve him well throughout his life.

Douglas was in his second year at West Point. The academy was investigating charges of hazing, abuse of new cadets by upperclassmen. A former cadet had recently died of tuberculosis. While at West Point, he was forced by older students to drink

Douglas MacArthur went on to be one of
West Point's most famous graduates.

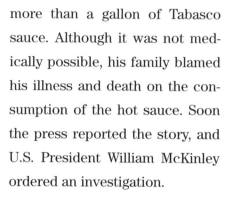

Founded in 1802, West Point stands as the oldest military college in the United States. Originally a male-only school, it began admitting women in 1976.

more than a gallon of Tabasco sauce. Although it was not medically possible, his family blamed his illness and death on the consumption of the hot sauce. Soon the press reported the story, and U.S. President William McKinley ordered an investigation.

The officers questioned Douglas about his own hazing experience. That summer, Douglas had been forced to repeatedly squat and rise over broken glass. Douglas remembered doing more than 200 of these "spread eagles" before he finally collapsed. He was then allowed to return to his tent, but his legs continued to shake uncontrollably for some time.

The court wanted a clear description of what had happened to Douglas. And they wanted names. Douglas had a difficult decision to make. Should he fully answer all of the board's questions and become known as the school informant? Or should he hold back and risk being thrown out of school?

Douglas thought about the two principles his parents had taught him from the time he was a child—to never lie and to never tattle. Later, he reflected on his decision. "Come what may, I would be no tattletale."

He would try to protect both his reputation with

his classmates and his future at West Point. When questioned, he only revealed the names of classmates who had already confessed or been expelled. He desperately hoped the officers would not give him a direct order to name the offenders.

"And then the order came, short, peremptory, unequivocal," he remembered. It was after that order that Douglas showed his nervousness and uncertainty:

> *At the end I grew weak and pleaded for mercy: that my whole life's hope lay in being an officer, that always I had been with the colors; that my father, then on the battleline 10,000 miles away, was their comrade-in-arms of the Civil and Indian wars; that I would do anything in the way of punishment, but not to strip me of my uniform. And then—I could not go on—*

The campus at West Point in the early 1900s

I heard the old soldier who presided say, "Court is recessed. Take him to his quarters."

Douglas was relieved to not be called to testify again. The court got the names from other sources. Shortly after the investigation concluded, West Point put anti-hazing rules into effect. Douglas' careful handling of his predicament won him the respect of his fellow students. Throughout his life and service in the military, he would win the respect of many more people, both in the United States and abroad.

Douglas, who became a general in the U.S. Army, is remembered by many as the greatest military leader in United States history. He wore an Army uniform for more than 50 years, including his years at West Point, and his service spanned three major wars.

His military career took him around the world. Kings and emperors knew him so well that they shared their hopes and dreams with him. At the conclusion of World War II, he was appointed a country's leader as well—taking the helm of the defeated nation of Japan and helping to build it into a free society.

Douglas was both incredibly brave and confident in his own abilities. While these traits led him to design risky, yet successful, military strategies, they also made him many enemies. Nevertheless, when he finally returned home after many years

A World War II poster, which featured the popular general, was used to show support for U.S. troops.

abroad, he was welcomed and praised for all he had done fighting to win his nation's wars.

Douglas MacArthur's role as an American hero seemed to have been written long before he was even born. His father, Arthur MacArthur Jr., was also a general in the Army. Douglas knew of no other life but the military, and he wanted nothing more than to serve his country.

2 THE SON OF A MILITARY MAN

❦

Douglas MacArthur grew up in a family of patriots who valued tradition. He adored his grandfather. A big, handsome man, Arthur MacArthur Sr. was filled with energy and loved to tell stories. Douglas could listen to him for hours.

Arthur Sr. immigrated to the United States from Scotland and served in the Massachusetts militia. He married the daughter of a wealthy business owner, and the couple had two sons. The family later settled in Milwaukee, Wisconsin.

When he was 15, Arthur MacArthur Jr. attended a private military school, where he learned about the skills and strategies of being a soldier. His teachers encouraged him to explore the possibility of attending the U.S. Military Academy at West Point,

Arthur MacArthur Jr. was awarded the Medal of Honor for his service during the Civil War.

New York. Admittance into West Point was fiercely competitive. Only a certain number of students could enroll each year. Armed with a letter of recommendation from the governor of Wisconsin, Arthur Jr. and his escort, a Wisconsin senator, went to the White House in May 1862, seeking appointment to the school by the president. Unfortunately, President Abraham Lincoln—who was Arthur Jr.'s hero—said all the presidential appointments to West Point for the coming year had already been filled.

So at the age of 17, Arthur Jr. joined the 24th Wisconsin Volunteer Infantry and went off to fight in the Civil War. He survived many bloody battles and was recognized for his bravery. Before he was 20, Arthur Jr. earned the rank of colonel, making him the youngest man in the Union Army to attain such a high post.

In February 1866, after the Civil War had ended, he headed west to the Indian wars on the American frontier. At this time, the first transcontinental railroad was being built to connect the Union Pacific in Omaha, Nebraska, with the Central Pacific in

Sacramento, California. Since the railroad was cut-
ting through the traditional lands of Native
Americans, it was Arthur Jr.'s job to make sure
Indians didn't harm the track or those working on it.

Arthur MacArthur Jr. sits at the far right with other Civil War commanders.

The West, in those days, was home to gun-
slingers, famed robbers, and legendary lawmen.
"He was at the center of the disorder, the violence,
the fighting involved in this drama of undisciplined
and untamed men," Douglas said of his father's
experience.

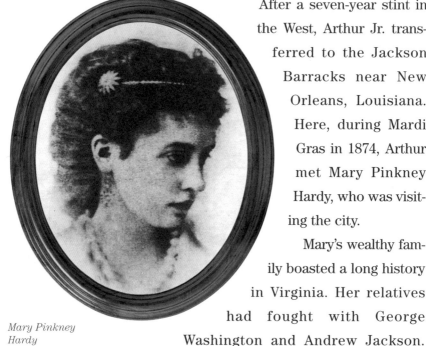

Mary Pinkney Hardy

After a seven-year stint in the West, Arthur Jr. transferred to the Jackson Barracks near New Orleans, Louisiana. Here, during Mardi Gras in 1874, Arthur met Mary Pinkney Hardy, who was visiting the city.

Mary's wealthy family boasted a long history in Virginia. Her relatives had fought with George Washington and Andrew Jackson. During the Civil War, her brothers had served under Confederate leader Robert E. Lee. "It was love at first sight, a love which lasted throughout their lives—thirty-seven years of perfect union," Douglas said about his parents.

Mary and Arthur Jr. married on May 19, 1875. They welcomed their first son, Arthur III, into the world in 1876. Two years later, Malcolm was born, and on January 26, 1880, in Little Rock, Arkansas, Douglas joined the family.

Five months after Douglas' birth, the MacArthurs moved to Fort Wingate, New Mexico. Because Arthur Jr. served in the military, the

MacArthur family moved around frequently. Douglas never knew any other kind of life.

"My earliest memory is the sound of Army bugles," he later wrote.

In 1883, all three MacArthur boys came down with measles. Arthur III and Douglas recovered, but 4-year-old Malcolm died. His death hit Mary hard, and she clung to her two remaining sons even more than she had in the past. Throughout her life, Mary remained extremely close to Douglas.

The following year, Arthur Jr. and the men he commanded marched 300 miles (480 kilometers) to Fort Selden, New Mexico. About 60 miles (96 km) north of

Douglas MacArthur (far left) was 5 years old in this family portrait.

As the son of a U.S. Army general, Douglas lived in cities throughout the country.

El Paso, Texas, the fort served as the guard post of the Rio Grande. Arthur's men were responsible for keeping the river area safe from attacks by Geronimo and his Apache warriors.

The MacArthur family joined Arthur Jr. in Fort Selden, and the post proved to be the first home Douglas remembered. Here, his father taught him how to ride a horse and shoot guns. Douglas and his brother also practiced marching and memorized Army rules. Both boys loved to read, too.

Douglas gravitated toward books about military history and heroes.

Because Fort Selden had no school, Mary taught her two sons, with some help from her husband. Their lessons covered the basics such as reading, writing, and math, as well as instructions on how to be good people. "We were to do what was right no matter what the personal sacrifice might be," Douglas remembered. "Our country was always to come first. Two things we must never do: never lie, never tattle."

The MacArthurs moved to Fort Leavenworth, Kansas, in 1886, and Douglas attended his first regular school. He proved to be a poor student. He didn't like to study and was distracted by the many events of the military community.

In 1889, Arthur Jr. was transferred to Washington, D.C., where Douglas would finish elementary school. The capital city lacked the excitement of Douglas' previous homes. He was often bored and showed little interest in his school work. Meanwhile, his brother excelled. Arthur III earned a spot at the Naval Academy in Annapolis, Maryland, in 1892 and graduated four years later.

Normally a healthy, athletic young man, Douglas' brother, Arthur III, would die unexpectedly when his appendix burst in 1923 at the age of 47. Douglas admitted in his autobiography that his death left a hole in his life that never again would be filled.

Douglas (wearing number 96) was a member of the undefeated 1896 West Texas Military Academy football team.

Toward the end of 1893, Arthur Jr. was transferred to Fort Sam Houston in San Antonio, Texas. Douglas was excited to be moving to one of the Army's most important posts. While there, Douglas attended West Texas Military Academy. It was here that a love of knowledge took hold of Douglas. Now 13 years old, he wanted to learn more about the world, and his grades improved. By the end of his first year, he was the school's star student.

Douglas also found a starring role on the school's sports teams. He played shortstop on the baseball team, led the football team as its quarterback, and earned championships in tennis. "I had always loved athletics and the spirit of competition moved me to participate in as many sports as possible," Douglas said.

Douglas loved Texas, so it was a disappointment when his father was transferred to St. Paul, Minnesota, at the beginning of 1897. "It was a wrench to leave San Antonio," Douglas said. "My four years there were without a doubt the happiest of my life."

But Douglas and his mother never lived in Minnesota. Instead, they moved to Milwaukee, Wisconsin. There a congressman had an opening for an appointment to West Point—the academy his father had hoped to attend—and Douglas needed to live there in order to be eligible to take the required test. Arthur Jr. visited his son and wife in Milwaukee on weekends.

While in Milwaukee, Douglas and his mother lived in Plankinton House hotel. Each day, Douglas walked two miles (3.2 km) to school and studied hard to prepare for the West Point exam. When the testing day finally arrived, Douglas felt ill, but his mother tried to make him feel better with comforting words of support:

Doug, you'll win if you don't lose your nerve. You must believe in yourself, my son, or no one else will believe in you. Be self-confident, self-reliant, and even if you don't make it, you will know you have done your best.

Douglas remembered his mother's words as he took the test. She proved right. He earned the best grade of all the young men taking the test that day, which secured him the opening at West Point.

The year 1898 turned out to be another year of change for the MacArthurs. The United States declared war on Spain in April in an effort to free Cuba from Spanish rule. During the course of the war, it became clear that Spain could not maintain its control over the Philippines, and the United States moved to seize the southeast Asian country.

That summer, Arthur Jr. traveled to the islands to help the cause. Douglas wanted to join him, but his father said he'd find plenty of chances for glory in the future. Right now, Douglas' education should stand as his first priority.

The war between the United States and Spain ended with a treaty that granted Cuba its freedom. Spain surrendered Guam, Puerto Rico, and the Philippines to the United States. The United States paid Spain $20 million for the Philippine islands. The Philippines remained a commonwealth of the United States until 1946, when it gained its independance.

Douglas obeyed his father and entered West Point on June 13, 1899. Little did he know that the Philippines would still play a huge part in his future. ✑

Arthur MacArthur Jr. (second from left) with his staff in the Philippines

3 TRAVELS AS A YOUNG OFFICER

ഗ⌒⌒ൟ

During the four years he attended West Point, Douglas worked hard to earn good grades, but he also found time to play. He socialized with friends and went to dances. The handsome young man caught the eyes of many girls, and he gained popularity among his classmates, as well.

Again, he put a great deal of energy into athletics, competing on many teams and earning a letter in baseball. At 5 feet 10 inches (178 centimeters) and 140 pounds (63 kilograms), he was not big enough to compete on the academy's football team. Instead, he served as team manager.

Douglas grew even closer to his mother during his years at West Point. With his father in the Philippines and his brother, Arthur III, sailing the

As a cadet, Douglas would occasionally sneak off academy grounds to visit his mother.

seas as a naval officer, Mary decided to live in West Point, where she could be near Douglas. When he wasn't at school, Douglas spent whatever time he could spare with his beloved mother. "Every night after supper, he spent a half hour with his mother," Douglas' first West Point roommate, Arthur Hyde, remembered. "If he could not get off the grounds, his mother would meet him and they would walk up and down in front of the barracks."

During his fourth year at West Point, Douglas was appointed cadet first captain, indicating his potential as a strong leader. This position made him the cadet commander over all of the cadets. At the end of his four years there, Douglas boasted the highest grade-point average of any student in the school's history. And on June 11, 1903, his parents watched with pride as he accepted his diploma and was commissioned a second lieutenant in the Army's Corp of Engineers.

After graduation, Douglas headed to San Francisco, California, where his father was commander of the many units in the Army's Department of the Pacific. Douglas wanted to spend some time with his parents before heading to the Philippines, his first assignment.

In the Philippines, Douglas surveyed land and worked on improvements to Manila harbor. The job was difficult and sometimes dangerous. When he

The newly commissioned second lieutenant shortly after his graduation from West Point

needed lumber to build docks or piers, he found it readily available—in the jungle. One time, he took a small group of men into the jungle to cut trees for lumber and almost didn't make it back. Along a narrow trail, the men were confronted by two guerrilla fighters. One of the fighters shot at Douglas with his rifle. The shot missed Douglas, but not his hat, which had a hole blazed straight through it. The enemy would not get another shot fired. Douglas, who always carried a pistol, raised his weapon and returned fire, killing the two men.

In April 1904, Douglas earned a promotion to first lieutenant. A few months later, he was diagnosed with two infections that were common in the jungle—malaria and ringworm. Sent home to the United States to recover, he was assigned to the district engineer's office in San Francisco. There he helped patrol Golden Gate harbor.

He also served on the California Debris Commission, which oversaw gold mining in the area. Remembering the rides he took to supervise the area, he said, "These duties were pleasant ones, especially the stagecoach trips through the Strawberry Valley that recalled my early days in the West." He enjoyed this position's responsibilities, and he grew stronger physically with each day he spent in California.

After gold was discovered in California in 1848, people rushed to the area to seek their fortunes. In less than a year, the population of the small port city of San Francisco grew to more than 25,000 people.

Douglas worked in California for about a year before being assigned to work with his father, who was in Japan assessing that country's war against Russia. Douglas was excited about this assignment. He had recently applied to be a war observer in Japan but was turned down because of a lack of experience. He would be serving as his father's aide, a position for which he was well-qualified.

"The purpose of our observations was to measure the strength of the Japanese Army and its methods of warfare," Douglas said. The military strength of Japan was of great concern to leaders in Washington, D.C., who were worried that the country might be a threat to American security in the future.

While in Japan, Douglas met all the great Japanese military commanders and witnessed first-hand the great devotion Japanese soldiers had for their emperor. Douglas, along with his parents, traveled throughout Asia, meeting with kings and other important leaders who shared details of their military operations with the American soldiers.

Douglas' appreciation of life in the United States deepened through his experiences in Asia. "We rubbed elbows with millions of the underprivileged who ... were interested only in getting a little more food in their stomachs, a little better coat on their backs, a little stronger roof over their heads," he said. He began to envision better education programs and a stronger economy for the Asian people, and he felt great hope for the people he'd met.

> *Many formal dinners were enjoyed during the MacArthurs' travels through Asia. At one such event, hosted by the king of Siam, the lights suddenly went out. Douglas was the night's hero when he simply changed a fuse. The king wished to promptly award him with a medal for his actions, but the young lieutenant declined.*

While Douglas traveled the world, he'd had little contact with political leaders in the United States. That changed in the fall of 1906. Douglas found himself back in the United States, attending a military engineering school, as required by the Army. He was named an assistant to U.S. President Theodore Roosevelt's military aide. The president himself requested MacArthur for the assignment. "The assignment proved of the greatest interest to me since I came into close contact for the first time with the leading political figures of the country," said Douglas.

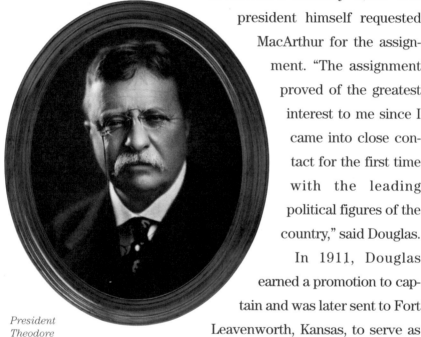

In 1911, Douglas earned a promotion to captain and was later sent to Fort Leavenworth, Kansas, to serve as head of the engineering department at the school there.

President Theodore Roosevelt

The following year, Douglas suffered a huge loss. His father had retired in 1909 and moved back home to Milwaukee with his wife. On September 5, 1912, Arthur Jr.'s old regiment planned its 50th reunion. Although he felt ill and the weather was unbearably hot, Arthur Jr. did not want to let his

Douglas MacArthur in Virginia while attending military engineering school

men down and insisted on attending. At the reunion, he rose to speak. The strain from the heat and his illness proved too much. The general's face turned white, and he collapsed and died. He was 67. No one could do anything to help him.

"My whole world changed that night," Douglas remembered. "Never have I been able to heal the wound in my heart." For the rest of his life, Douglas carried a framed photo of his father with him wherever he traveled. ✥

4 BATTLE-TESTED

Chapter

‿◌‿

Douglas wanted to serve his country on the battle-field, like the father he so admired. It wouldn't be long before he got the chance.

With his father's death, however, Douglas felt a deeper responsibility to look after his mother, Mary. So when he was sent to Washington, D.C., shortly after his father's death, he brought his mother with him.

In September 1913, MacArthur was named a member of the General Staff, a select group of 38 officers in Washington that he later described as "the brains of the Army in planning operations and deciding matters of highest importance." Douglas made many important contacts through this job, meeting the top officers in both the Army and Navy.

In an effort to stand out from his fellow soldiers, MacArthur often strayed from military dress codes.

Victoriano Huerta ruled Mexico for less than nine months.

About this time, the United States started having problems with neighboring Mexico. General Victoriano Huerta had seized power in Mexico and began arresting and harassing Americans who were legally visiting the country. U.S. President Woodrow Wilson decided to take action. U.S. ships were sent to blockade the Mexican port at Veracruz, and on April 21, 1914, American troops took control of the city. Soon after, Huerta fled his country.

During this time, MacArthur was sent to Veracruz to learn more about the area and report back to military officials, who wanted to be prepared should the field army be called to serve. MacArthur's dress, during these days in the field, began to relax from the standard-issue Army uniform. He liked setting himself apart from others and could often be seen wearing a long cardigan sweater accented by a bold silk scarf around his neck.

After completing his duty in Mexico in September 1914, MacArthur was promoted to the rank of major and again was asked to serve on the General Staff in Washington, D.C. But before long, the United States faced more trouble—this time in Europe, where World War I raged.

The war broke out after the June 28, 1914, assassination of Archduke Franz Ferdinand and his wife, Sophie, of Austria-Hungary. Officials in Austria-Hungary held their old rival—the government of Serbia—responsible for Ferdinand's death. After Austria-Hungary declared war on their enemy, other European countries joined the fight. Soon, the Allies—France, Great Britain, and Russia—

This photo of Archduke Ferdinand and his wife, Sophie, was taken one hour before their assassination.

faced off against the Central Powers—Austria-Hungary and Germany. More countries joined both sides of the fight as hostilities dragged on.

The United States had hoped to avoid war, but Germans angered Americans when they started sinking unarmed U.S. ships in 1915. Then in early 1917, British forces intercepted and decoded a message that revealed a German plan to persuade Mexico to go to war against the United States. By

April 6, 1917, U.S. officials had had enough and declared war on Germany.

Now a colonel, MacArthur joined the infantry and became chief of staff of the 42nd Division. He had long dreamed of fighting on the front lines with an infantry, and, as he told a reporter, those who served overseas during the war would receive the highest promotions. In the fall of 1917, MacArthur and the 42nd Division headed to France to fight the Germans.

At first, the men spent time training in eastern France, but MacArthur was eager to join the fighting. On February 26, 1918, he got his chance. He talked French General Georges de Bazelaire into letting him join a French army raiding party to free prisoners captured by the Germans. MacArthur thought that seeing the actual battlefields of war would help him form stronger battle plans for when he led his own men into battle. He explained:

> *MacArthur helped establish the 42nd Division. It was known as the Rainbow Division because its members came from across the United States. Usually, divisions were made up of soldiers from just one state or small area of the country. The 27,000 men in the Rainbow Division came from 26 different states and the District of Columbia.*

> *It is all very well to make a perfect plan of attack, to work out in theory a foolproof*

design for victory. But if that plan does not
consider the caliber of troops, the terrain to
be fought over, the enemy strength opposed,
then it may become confused and fail.

The French general knew MacArthur spoke the
truth. "I told him frankly, 'I cannot fight them if I cannot see them,'" MacArthur said. "He understood, and told me to go."

With faces camouflaged with soot, MacArthur

and the French raiders set out in the middle of the night. They trudged through the mud and cut through the German's lines of barbed wire. They had nearly reached their destination when a German guard heard their approach and began firing his gun toward them.

The gunshots sounded as an alarm for the other Germans, who quickly joined in the shooting. The raiders fought in hand-to-hand combat with their enemy and finally secured the prisoners' release. Their mission proved to be a success, and the battle-tested MacArthur earned the respect of the French soldiers.

MacArthur carefully studied the raid and its aftermath to ensure that he knew what to expect when his troops entered the war. He went to a French field hospital to see how the wounded were cared for in the field. He also observed the questioning of German soldiers who were captured and carefully analyzed all the events of the skirmish.

Having gained this experience, he readied to take his own men into battle. It was a cold drizzling night when the 42nd Division set out on its first mission. The Germans were quick to fire, and the division's casualties began to mount. MacArthur was concerned about the inexperience of his men. "I began to feel uneasy," he remembered. "They were not professionals. Few of them had ever been under

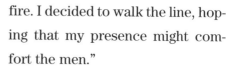

During World War I, Douglas MacArthur used skills his father had shared from his experience in fighting in the Indian wars on the frontier. One trick he learned and used often was crawling toward the enemy to avoid being shot.

fire. I decided to walk the line, hoping that my presence might comfort the men."

His fearlessness inspired his men and gave them the courage to fight back. By the end of the battle, they had proven their bravery and ability. Once the 42nd entered the war, they had little relief. The division fought almost continually for 82 days.

MacArthur kept in contact with his mother through the war, writing her often to let her know where he and the division had been. Mary, who had kept a scrapbook of her son's service since his first fieldwork in Veracruz, kept all clippings of her son from American newspapers.

On July 4, MacArthur and his men joined the French 4th Army led by General Henri Gouraud. MacArthur had heard of this French war hero long before he met him, but he "was not prepared for the heroic figure to whom [he] reported:"

> *With one arm gone, and half a leg missing, with his red beard glittering in the sunlight, the jaunty rake of his cocked hat and the oratorical brilliance of his resonant voice, his impact was overwhelming. ... And he was just as good as he looked.*

After learning of a German plan to attack the 4th Army line, Gouraud decided his men would surprise the enemy. The French and American soldiers attacked first, opening with an overwelming force of fire from more than 2,500 guns. "The artillery fire could be heard in Paris, nearly 100 miles [160 km] away," MacArthur said.

French General Henri Gouraud

The Germans recovered from their shock and fought back, but the battle proved to be a turning point in the war. The French, Americans, and the rest of the Allies continued to earn victories against the Germans and the other Central Powers.

On November 11, 1918, the Germans agreed to an armistice, or a cease-fire.

Having proved his courage and skill in battle, MacArthur earned a promotion to general. As a senior officer, he wasn't required to follow the same rules as the soldiers. Instead of carrying a weapon, MacArthur held a riding crop in his hands, a habit he picked up from his years in the West. He refused to wear a helmet because it hurt his head. And,

MacArthur was 37 years old in this photograph taken in France during World War I.

unlike the rest of the troops, he never carried a gas mask. He said the mask hampered his movements. Like the long sweater and colorful scarf from his Veracruz days, his unique appearance also set him apart from other officers, a benefit he enjoyed.

It wasn't just his appearance that set him apart. MacArthur was well-respected for his leadership during the war, and many soldiers who worked with him showered him with praise. His Rainbow Division, as one of the top U.S. divisions in the war, was also praiseworthy. The division had some of the highest numbers of German prisoners captured, enemy ground taken, and medals awarded.

MacArthur himself received two Distinguished Service Crosses, a Distinguished Service Medal, six Silver Stars, and two wound stripes. About a year and a half after leaving to fight in Europe, the decorated war hero returned home to face a new challenge in a place he knew well. ॐ

5 FIGHTING TO MAINTAIN MILITARY MIGHT

Chapter

❦

Douglas MacArthur reacted with surprise when General Peyton March, the Army's chief of staff, asked him to serve as superintendent of West Point. "I'm not an educator," he said. "I'm a field soldier. Besides, there are so many of my old professors there. I can't do it."

Yet, March, his father's old friend, convinced him otherwise. The school needed a military man with experience in modern battle to update the program. March told him that the school was 40 years behind the times. The academic board at West Point wished to hold on to its traditions and was hesitant to make changes to the program. March saw MacArthur as the right man to lead the school's modernization.

Edward, the Prince of Wales, (left) toured the West Point campus in 1920 with MacArthur as his guide.

MacArthur's belief in the importance of physical training is still felt at West Point. A MacArthur quote is inscribed on the academy's gymnasium wall: "Upon the fields of friendly strife are sown the seeds that upon other fields, on other days, will bear the fruits of victory."

MacArthur took the job in 1919 and worked hard to ensure the education and training at West Point would prepare cadets for battles they would face in the field. Under his leadership, all cadets were now required to take part in athletics. MacArthur knew troops had to be in good physical shape to withstand the rigors of war, and athletics helped strengthen and train the body.

MacArthur also updated West Point's science and military classes and required cadets to learn more about history and world events. He encouraged the academy's instructors to take continuing education classes at some of the best colleges in the country and to share what they learned with the cadets.

But MacArthur didn't spend all of his time working. At a West Point social event, he met the woman who would become his first wife.

When he first saw Henriette Louise Cromwell Brooks, MacArthur couldn't take his eyes off her. Drawn to her beauty, he soon learned she hated her first name and preferred to be called Louise. He also found out that Louise was divorced and had two children. Louise thoroughly charmed the young

Louise was a wealthy woman. This 1925 photo of her and Douglas was taken at Rainbow Hill, her large estate near Baltimore, Maryland.

general. In a case of love at first sight, they became engaged that evening. "If he hadn't proposed the first time we met, I believe I would have done it myself," Louise later said.

On February 14, 1922, six months after they met, the couple married. But General John Pershing, who was now chief of staff of the Army, was angry about the marriage. Before becoming engaged to MacArthur, Louise had been seeing one of Pershing's aides, a man Pershing loved like a son. The breakup didn't sit well with Pershing, so he removed MacArthur from West Point and reassigned him to service in the Philippines.

Louise hated life in the Philippines. She was often lonely and bored. While other officers' wives socialized together, Louise did little to try and make friends. In fact, she often did just the opposite, starting with the day they left for the Philippines. Because MacArthur was the highest-ranking officer on the ship, his family's items were loaded onto the vessel first. Louise brought so much luggage that no one else was allowed more than one trunk, making her quite unpopular.

In the years that followed, Louise continued to make enemies of the officers' wives. She finally moved back to New York in 1927. Two years later, the couple divorced.

Big changes were also brewing in the United States. The stock market crashed in 1929, and the country slipped into the Great Depression. Millions of people lost their jobs as banks failed and factories closed. Many people were forced to rely on government help to survive.

As the American people suffered, Congress looked for ways to save money. Since the country was now at peace, the military budget appeared to be an area where Congress could make cutbacks and save money. But with Japan threatening further expansion and Germany gaining strength,

Photographer Russell Lee captured the struggles of rural Americans during the Great Depression. A 1939 photo shows a migrant family resting on folded cots.

MacArthur, who returned to the United States to serve as chief of staff of the Army in August 1930, believed Congress was making a huge mistake. His job now offered him the opportunity to tell lawmakers what he thought. He warned congressmen and the public that the threat of another war was real, but many refused to believe him.

When a vote came before Congress to reduce the number of men in the officer corps from 12,255 to 10,255, MacArthur quickly stepped forward to express his alarm:

> *An army can live on short rations; it can be insufficiently clothed and housed; it can even be poorly armed and equipped;*

but in action it is doomed to destruction without the trained and adequate leadership of officers.

To MacArthur's relief, the lawmakers listened to him and narrowly defeated the bill. But more battles lurked on the horizon. Some of the

President Franklin D. Roosevelt

most stressful would be with U.S. President Franklin D. Roosevelt, who had been elected in 1932.

When the new president took his first oath of office, he started a series of social programs to get Americans back to work. While Roosevelt concentrated on strengthening the U.S. economy, MacArthur grew angry that the military budget seemed likely to be cut. In a meeting with the president, MacArthur let his temper get the best of him. Though he usually spoke his mind, he knew he'd gone too far this time:

The country's safety was at stake, and I said so bluntly. The President turned the full vials of his sarcasm upon me. ... The tension began to boil over. ... In my emotional exhaustion I spoke recklessly and said something to the general effect that when we lost the next war, and an American boy, lying in the mud with an enemy bayonet through his belly and an enemy foot on his dying throat, spat out his last curse, I wanted the name not to be MacArthur, but Roosevelt.

MacArthur immediately realized he shouldn't have talked to the president this way. He apologized and offered to resign as chief of staff. Roosevelt told him his job was safe. But the whole incident left MacArthur feeling sick. He left the meeting, went outside, and threw up on the White House steps.

As chief of staff, MacArthur continued to fight for funding to keep the U.S. military strong. Despite German advances in Europe, the president and Congress remained optimistic about avoiding war. But they would soon see that the country's experience in World War I would pale in comparison to what lay ahead.

In 1924, Congress passed a law promising veterans of World War I bonuses that would be paid in 1945. During the Great Depression, many veterans found themselves in desperate need of the money much sooner. In June 1932, around 15,000 veterans, known as the Bonus Army, came to Washington, D.C., to pressure Congress to release the money. When a bill asking for early payment of the bonuses failed to pass, the veterans became angry. MacArthur was given the duty of clearing the troops out of Washington, D.C., making him an unpopular person at that time.

Chapter 6

A Second World War Erupts

❧❧❧

After finishing his term as chief of staff in 1935, Douglas MacArthur again found himself in the Philippines. President Roosevelt sent him to serve as an adviser on national defense to the Philippines' president-elect, Manuel Quezon. Because the Philippines was an American commonwealth, the responsibility of its defense fell to the United States. In 1946, the Philippines would be gaining independence, as well as the responsibility of defending itself. The commonwealth needed to prepare for this responsibility, and MacArthur would offer leadership in the planning.

Though MacArthur's mother hadn't been feeling well for years, she chose to go to the Philippines with her son. About two months after they arrived in

German soldiers advance after invading Poland in September 1939.

Manila, Mary died. MacArthur was filled with grief. Always a devoted son, he kept the memory of his mother close. He carried her walking stick with him and read from her Bible each night.

MacArthur threw himself into his work to cope with his loss. He helped establish a military academy to train Filipino officers and devised a plan for defense in which each portion of the small country would be responsible for supplying a certain number of soldiers.

MacArthur also found comfort with a new love. On the way to Manila, he'd met a beautiful young woman named Jean Marie Faircloth. The American woman was on her way to Shanghai, China, to stay with some friends. Jean and Douglas often shared breakfast on the ship, until they arrived at MacArthur's destination at Manila and parted ways. When Jean reached Shanghai, she turned right around and headed back to Manila to be near the general.

The couple married in New York City on April 30, 1937. "It was perhaps the smartest thing I have ever done. She has been my constant friend, sweetheart, and devoted supporter ever since," MacArthur said of his marriage.

The couple returned to the Philippines, where they lived in the penthouse apartment in the Manila Hotel. Of the apartment's seven rooms, the library was most cherished. There were almost 2,000 books on the shelves—some of which had belonged to

Jean and Douglas MacArthur on their wedding day

MacArthur's father. Both MacArthur's and his father's military medals were on display in the room as well.

On February 21, 1938, Douglas and Jean welcomed their first and only child into the world. Following the MacArthur family tradition, they named him Arthur. Junior, as Arthur IV was called, brought much joy to his father. Together, they sang Army songs while the general shaved. And from the time Junior learned to walk, the two greeted each other every morning with a salute, followed by a

Adolf Hitler

march together around the general's bedroom.

While MacArthur's family enjoyed life in the Philippines, the events that the general had feared began to unfold in Europe. On September 1, 1939, Nazi Germany, headed by Adolf Hitler, attacked Poland. Two days later, the Allies, France and Great Britain, declared war on Germany, sparking the beginning of World War II. Shocking the world with their speed and military might, German forces invaded and seized Denmark, Norway, Luxembourg, the Netherlands, Belgium, and France. When Italy entered the war in support of Germany in June 1940, the only European nation left fighting the German aggressors was Great Britain.

In the fall of 1940, Japan joined Germany and Italy in their fight. The three countries together became known at the Axis powers.

The Soviet Union entered the fight against the Axis powers when Germany invaded the country in June 1941. Then, on December 7, 1941, Japan bombed U.S. military bases in Pearl Harbor, Hawaii, and the United States was drawn into the war. When this shocking news reached MacArthur, he realized the Philippines also stood in danger. He knew the islands were unprepared for a Japanese attack.

The expected attack on the Phillipines came just hours after the bombing at Pearl Harbor. Every U.S. B-17 bomber at Clark Field northwest of Manila was either damaged or destroyed by 90 Japanese bombers. In addition, since the U.S. Navy's Pacific fleet had

The USS Arizona *burns after the bombing of Pearl Harbor.*

been all but wiped out at Pearl Harbor, no more ammunition, food, or troops would be able to come to the Philippines' aid. MacArthur badgered Washington for help. But he was disappointed to discover:

A 1941 map shows four areas where Japanese troops invaded the Philippines.

> *President Roosevelt and Prime Minister Churchill ... reaffirmed a policy to concentrate first on the defeat of Germany. Until victory was won in Europe, operations in the Pacific would be directed toward containing the Japanese with the limited resources available.*

BATTLE FOR MANILA

Japanese forces launched a number of small attacks on the Philippines before making a major assault on December 22. About 80,000 Japanese soldiers landed in the northwestern section of the Philippines—nearly twice as many troops as MacArthur had on the entire string of islands.

As more Japanese troops arrived, MacArthur and his men decided to move westward toward Manila and the Bataan Peninsula. This strategy kept his men from being encircled or split apart into a group in the north and a group in the south. But it also forced MacArthur's men to abandon nearly all their food and weapons.

It would only be a matter of time before MacArthur would have to surrender to the Japanese if aid didn't arrive soon. As disheartening as this was for MacArthur, it was more so for the people of the Philippines, who were aware of U.S. efforts in Europe. He said:

> *They were able to understand military failure, but the apparent disinterest on the part of the United States was incomprehensible. ... Their feelings ranged from bewilderment to revulsion.*

As MacArthur and his men hung on, the Japanese tried to crush their spirits. On January 10, 1942, the commander of the Japanese Expeditionary

Japanese General Masaharu Homma was later executed for the mistreatment of prisoners of war in the Philippines.

Force sent a message to MacArthur encouraging him to give up. When MacArthur ignored the message, the Japanese papered the ground with leaflets that told the troops they were doomed and that they should surrender since their leader refused to do so.

Yet the men continued to fight.

MacArthur couldn't help but admire the men's courage and commitment to keeping the Philippines out of enemy hands. He later wrote about the Filipino soldiers:

*They died hard—those savage men. ...
And around their necks, as we buried
them, would be a thread of dirty string
with its dangling crucifix. They were
filthy, and they were lousy, and they
stank. And I loved them.*

Then MacArthur received word that he was
being transferred to Australia. He tried his best to
ignore the order. However, his staff convinced him
to go. They told him that the men and weapons
being gathered in Australia could be used to rescue
the Philippines.

Despite his desire to stay in the Philippines and
fight until the end, MacArthur and his family—who
had been living on the small Philippine island of
Corregidor—left the islands with a few other officers on March 11, 1942, bound for Australia. As the
group traveled, MacArthur slept with his head on his
wife's shoulder. Jean told another member of the
traveling party that it was the first time her husband
had slept well since the attack on Pearl Harbor. 🐦

7 LEADING FROM AUSTRALIA

Chapter

ⓔⓧⓞ

Sixty reporters waited for the MacArthurs' arrival in Melbourne, Australia, on March 17, 1942. Douglas MacArthur, who was always eager to talk to the press, didn't shy away from any of the reporter's questions. He made it clear he still felt that the defeat of Japan should be a higher priority than the defeat of Germany. He also repeated a promise that he would return to help the Philippines.

Once in Australia, MacArthur hoped he'd be put in charge of the entire Pacific region, including the land, sea, and air forces. But he was only assigned to handle the war in the southwest Pacific.

In July, MacArthur's headquarters moved to Brisbane, Australia, 500 miles (800 km) north of Melbourne. He and his family settled in at Lennon's

MacArthur walks with American officers during an inspections trip in Australia in October 1942.

> MacArthur was grateful to his wife for making the 3,000-mile (4,800-km) trip from Corregidor to Melbourne. To show his appreciation, he bought her a watch and had it inscribed to read, "To my Bravest. Bataan–Corregidor, March 1942. MacArthur."

Hotel, where young Arthur made friends with the son of one of the hotel's assistant managers. Having his wife and son nearby helped keep MacArthur strong during the challenging times of war. He and his son kept their morning tradition of salutes and marches, but now the ritual was followed by the presentation of a small gift from father to son. MacArthur loved to spoil his son.

That summer, MacArthur, who was very popular with the American public at the time, was named Father of the Year back in the United States. He responded:

> *Nothing has touched me more deeply than the action of the National Fathers' Day Committee. By profession, I am a soldier and take pride in that fact, but I am prouder, infinitely prouder, to be a father. A soldier destroys in order to build; the father only builds, never destroys. … It is my hope my son, when I am gone, will remember me not from the battle but in the home.*

MacArthur didn't have time to bask in the glory of his award however. He quickly set to work

MacArthur was very protective of his son, Arthur. After Arthur broke his arm while ice skating, the general would no longer allow the boy to skate.

making plans to protect Australia from a Japanese invasion. Early in the war, the Japanese had gained control of many islands in the southwest Pacific. Now, the Japanese sat poised to take Australia. Many believed the best plan was to prepare Australia to defend itself, but MacArthur devised a bolder plan. He led American and Australian soldiers to retake the islands captured by the Japanese and push the enemy farther away.

Upset by the number of lives that were lost in directly challenging the Japanese soldiers in their

Liberating the islands of southeast Asia from Japanese control became MacArthur's main goal in 1942.

strongholds, MacArthur created a strategy he called island hopping. Under this plan, MacArthur's forces would attack a relatively weak area through which the Japanese received much-needed supplies. With the supply line cut, the strong area would soon suffer from lack of food, ammunition, and other things necessary for battle. MacArthur knew it was much easier to starve the enemy than to beat it outright in battle, and his strategy worked. One by one, MacArthur gained control of New Guinea, the Solomon Islands, and others areas held by the Japanese. Because the Australian and American troops were "hopping" from island to island, the Japanese troops never knew where they would be attacked next.

The island-hopping strategy relied on close cooperation between air and naval forces to isolate areas under enemy control. MacArthur possessed the unique ability to organize other nations and services to work together in these efforts.

MacArthur observes a military operation from a B-17 Flying Fortress gun port above New Guinea.

Every victory brought MacArthur closer to the Philippines, but not everyone agreed that the Philippines should be the United States' next priority. For one, Navy Admiral Chester Nimitz, the head of the war in the central Pacific, wanted to skip over the Philippines and fight in Formosa, now known as Taiwan.

In July 1944, MacArthur traveled to Pearl Harbor to meet with President Roosevelt and Nimitz. Roosevelt hadn't yet decided on the best strategy and asked each man to give his view of how the war in the Pacific should proceed. Afterward, Roosevelt took MacArthur aside and talked with him alone. As usual, MacArthur spoke his mind:

From left to right, MacArthur joins President Roosevelt, Navy Admiral William D. Leahy, and Nimitz at the 1944 meeting in Hawaii.

Mr. President, ... you hope to be reelected President of the United States, but the nation will never forgive you if you approve a plan which leaves 17 million Christian American subjects to wither in the Philippines ... until the peace treaty frees them. ... Politically, it would ruin you.

MacArthur didn't expect the president to take his advice, but he did. Roosevelt wrote to MacArthur, who had gone back to Australia: "I will push on that plan for I am convinced that as a whole that it is logical and can be done. Some day there will be a flag raising in Manila—and without a question I want you to do it." ℬ

8 THE TIDE TURNS

Chapter

ಿಂ⌘ೋ

The tide of the war had turned in the Allies' favor by the spring of 1943. In Europe, the Germans were being fought back in their attempt to control Russia, and the Italians faced certain defeat. In the Pacific, Japan was also dealing with defeats.

Though the United States still remained focused on defeating Hitler, MacArthur had never forgotten his promise to return to the Philippines. Now, with the president's support, MacArthur found himself bound for the islands again. When he landed on the beaches of Leyte in October 1944, he grabbed a microphone to announce his arrival. "People of the Philippines," he said triumphantly, "I have returned. By the grace of Almighty God, our forces stand again on Philippine soil."

MacArthur looks over the destruction at Clark Field after his return to the Philippines in 1944.

MacArthur wades through the water to reach the shores of Leyte upon his arrival.

A few months earlier, President-elect Quezon had died in the United States. Accompanied by the new Philippine president, Sergio Osmena, MacArthur urged the people of Leyte to fight for their freedom. "In the name of your sacred dead, strike!" MacArthur shouted. "Let no heart be faint. Let every arm be steeled."

Encouraged by MacArthur's return, the Philippine people were inspired to battle. The fight to regain the Philippines proved both difficult and emotional for MacArthur. This time, however, the soldiers' efforts were rewarded. In February 1945, MacArthur's troops took back the Bataan Peninsula, and Corregidor soon followed. As he again set foot on the small island he had once called home, MacArthur's emotions overcame him. "This visit is easing an ache that has been in my heart for three years," he said.

On February 7, MacArthur visited Bilibid Prison in Manila, where the Japanese had held some of the soldiers they'd captured. His eyes filled with tears at the sight of the prisoners, who looked like skeletons. The tired, worn men mustered smiles and joy at the sight of the general. "You made it," one of the men said to MacArthur. "I'm a little late, but we finally came," MacArthur replied.

Jean and Arthur IV returned to Manila in March. Jean spent much of her time visiting soldiers who were in hospitals throughout the Philippines.

When MacArthur arrived at Bilibid Prison, he found hundreds of American soldiers weak and starving.

Arthur, meanwhile, discovered a love for music. With the help of an English teacher, he learned to read music and could even play piano by ear.

In April 1945, President Roosevelt died, and his vice president, Harry Truman, became the country's leader. The war in Europe ended with the German surrender on May 7. Yet the Japanese refused to admit defeat.

Tired of the fighting, Truman and other Allied leaders looked to a new weapon to end the war—the atomic bomb, which created a huge explosion capable of massive destruction. Truman held no doubt that such a weapon would bring the war to an end. Truman, along with the United Kingdom and China, sent a message to Japan. The countries threatened to destroy Japan if it didn't surrender. Japan refused.

On August 6, 1945, a U.S. bomber dropped an atomic bomb on Hiroshima, Japan. When Japanese leaders made no move to surrender, another atomic bomb was dropped on August 9, this time on Nagasaki. The two bombs killed around 140,000 people. Four days later, the Japanese surrendered.

MacArthur made his way to Japan for the official surrender ceremony, where he would again see one of his old friends. When MacArthur had left the

Philippines for Australia, he placed General Jonathan Wainwright in charge of the fight in the Philippines. Wainwright and his men held on for as long as they could, but in May 1942, they were forced to surrender to Japanese troops. Now at the end of World War II, Wainwright stood among those released from Japanese prison camps.

MacArthur embraces Jonathan Wainwright at their reunion at the New Grand Hotel in Yokohama, Japan.

Three years in the camps took a heavy toll on Wainwright. MacArthur's eyes filled with tears when he saw his friend, who looked terribly thin and much older than the last time the two generals had seen each other. After the two men hugged, Wainwright, his eyes filled with pain, said he expected he wouldn't be welcome in the U.S. Army again because of what he saw as failure on his part. MacArthur couldn't believe his ears. He knew Wainwright had been put in a situation where he had no chance of winning. "Why, Jim, you can have command of a corps whenever you want it!" MacArthur reassured his friend.

On September 2, 1945, MacArthur formally accepted the Japanese surrender on the USS *Missouri*. The war in the Pacific had officially ended, but the rebuilding process was about to begin. During the surrender ceremony, MacArthur said:

> *It is my earnest hope and indeed the hope of all mankind that from this solemn occasion a better world shall emerge out of the blood and carnage of the past—a world founded upon faith and understanding—a world dedicated to the dignity of man and the fulfillment of his most cherished wish—for freedom, tolerance, and justice.*

MacArthur, who was made the supreme commander of the Allied forces in August 1945, was now responsible for helping Japan become a democratic nation. The country faced the daunting task of rebuilding. More than 1.27 million Japanese died during the final four years of World War II. "Never in history had a nation and its people been more completely crushed," MacArthur said.

Less than a week after Japan's official surrender, MacArthur arrived in the country's capital after a sad journey through a torn and tattered landscape. "It was just 22 miles [35 km] from the New Grand Hotel in Yokohama to the American Embassy, which was to be my home ... but they were 22 miles of devastation and vast piles of charred rubble," MacArthur remembered. From this rubble, MacArthur helped Japan begin anew. He said:

The torn remains of the Museum of Science and Industry stand in Hiroshima a few days after the dropping of the atomic bomb.

Because I had been given so much power, I was faced with the most difficult situation of my life. Power is one thing. The problem of how to administer it is another. I had to rebuild a nation that had been almost completely destroyed by the war.

As one of his first acts, MacArthur destroyed Japan's military capability to ensure another war wouldn't be on the horizon. Then he led the rebuilding of bombed factories, worked to improve the country's educational system, and set up a health department to ward off epidemics of typhoid, smallpox, and other deadly diseases. He also helped the country establish

This photograph captured MacArthur's meeting with Emperor Hirohito in 1945. It was published in Japanese newspapers.

a new government and hold free elections.

As he moved Japan toward a more democratic way of life, MacArthur tried to remain respectful of Japanese tradition and culture, and he agreed to

Hirohito continued to serve as the emperor of Japan until his death in 1989.

meet with Emperor Hirohito. MacArthur wanted to ensure the emperor continued to be treated with dignity, though he now stood as more of a ceremonial symbol than as an absolute ruler. "He played a major role in the spiritual regeneration of Japan, and his loyal co-operation and influence had much to do with the success of the occupation," MacArthur recalled.

As always, Jean and Arthur, who was nearly 8 years old, lived with the general in Japan. Arthur often felt lonely. There were few American children for him to play with, and he was rarely able to play like a normal child. His father—at 65 years of age— was far older than most fathers of young boys, and the general was often too busy to play with his son.

Rebuilding the war-torn country took years. By early 1950, Japan had traveled far down the road to recovery. However, MacArthur's attention soon would be drawn elsewhere. 🦢

Wonsan

Pyongyang

Seoul

Taejon

Yon

Poh

Pusan

9 KOREA

და

As MacArthur worked to rebuild Japan, trouble brewed in nearby Korea. Japan had taken control of Korea in 1910. When World War II came to an end, the United States and the Soviet Union took Korea away from the defeated nation. American troops occupied the southern portion of Korea, while the Soviet Union controlled the northern part.

In 1947, the United Nations said Korea should be reunited as one country and hold elections for its own government. Both the Soviet Union and the United States were to prepare to remove their troops from the area in the coming years.

The following year, South Koreans elected an anti-communist leader to power. A few months later, communists in North Korea created their own

Diagonal lines on a 1950 map indicate the land North Korea controlled in July of that year. The dashed line shows the original border.

government. Not willing to be reunited, both North Korea and South Korea laid claim to the whole country. Battles over this land dispute occasionally erupted, but a full-scale war broke out shortly after the United States pulled out its troops in 1949.

On June 25, 1950, North Korea invaded South Korea. MacArthur was awakened to the news, which brought back disturbing memories of when he heard the news that Pearl Harbor had been bombed.

On June 27, the United Nations stepped in and asked its members to come to South Korea's aid. The United States answered the U.N.'s call. MacArthur traveled to Korea to assess the situation and form a plan. President Truman ordered MacArthur to command all U.S. air, land, and sea operations in the defense of South Korea.

North Korea gained speed as it conquered much of South Korea. By the end of July, North Korea controlled 90 percent of South Korea. But in September, the tide turned. MacArthur had been pushing for an invasion by U.S. air, land, and sea forces at Inchon, a port city just west of Seoul, since his visit to Korea in June, but he was unable to find supporters for his idea. Inchon's harbor was plagued with violent currents and other natural disadvantages. But MacArthur knew the enemy would not expect an attack there. A victory at Inchon would put his forces in the position to push North Korea back out of South Korea. He issued a revised plan in September, and officials in Washington, D.C., gave him the necessary approval.

On September 13, MacArthur traveled to Sasebo, Japan, where he would command forces during the attack. While he traveled, he saw a huge rainbow stretching across the sky. Remembering his beloved Rainbow Division from World War II, he saw the arch as a sign that the invasion would be a success. Two days later, U.S. forces launched the invasion and

MacArthur observes the invasion of Inchon from the commanding ship.

> The *Korean War* ended July 27, 1953. While the United Nations and North Korea reached an agreement to cease hostilities, North and South Korea have never signed a formal peace treaty.

stunned their enemy, ending the string of North Korean victories. Historians often cite the Inchon landing as MacArthur's greatest military moment.

The war raged on for nearly three more years, but MacArthur wouldn't last that long. He openly criticized the U.S. government and its policies in fighting the war. MacArthur wanted to be granted the power to bomb parts of China, a fighting supporter of North Korea. However, officials in Washington, D.C., including President Truman, feared such bold measures could result in the start of World War III.

When he couldn't get approval to bomb China, MacArthur made his arguments public. In a national magazine, he said he couldn't effectively deal with the Chinese because of restrictions placed on him by leaders in Washington, D.C.

MacArthur's statements angered President Truman. To avoid similar embarrassments in the future, the president ordered military leaders to clear their comments with Washington officials before making public statements. But Truman would soon discover MacArthur wouldn't be silenced.

Despite their disagreements, Truman tried to

Truman and MacArthur met to discuss the progress of the war in October 1950. Despite the smiles, the men did not like each other. It was the first and last time the two met.

mend his relationship with MacArthur. He sent the general a long letter explaining the reasons behind the U.S. strategy in Korea. He ended the letter by saying how much MacArthur was appreciated.

MacArthur, however, accused Truman and his administration of deliberately trying to end the war with the two sides pretty much right back where they were at the start of the conflict. To MacArthur, this was unacceptable. Too many soldiers had suffered, and too many lives had been lost for what he considered a tie. He decided to send a message to the Chinese without consulting anyone in Washington. The message told the Chinese to either admit defeat or be destroyed.

President Truman flew into a rage. This message made it impossible for Truman to start peace talks. However, the American public generally responded with praise for MacArthur's action. They were tired of hearing only about bad news and defeats, and the general's bold note gave them cause to cheer. Because of the public reaction, Truman felt he couldn't fire MacArthur for his action, but the president would soon be presented with another chance.

MacArthur sent a letter to Speaker of the House Joseph Martin. In the letter, the general said he believed that if the United States lost this war to communism in Asia, Europe would be the next to fall. However, MacArthur said, if the communists were chased out of Korea, Europe would likely avoid a potential war against communists and remain free. He said that signing a truce with North Korea and the Chinese would prove to be a mistake. "There is no substitute for victory," he wrote.

On April 5, 1951, Martin read the letter on the floor of Congress. In addition, MacArthur granted interviews to British writers in which he clearly spoke his mind about restrictions placed on him in fighting the war. He criticized U.S. policy, but readers knew he was really criticizing the president. His actions directly disobeyed orders from his commander in chief, the president. Truman possessed all the ammunition he needed now. He

As illustrated in this 1951 cartoon, many Americans did not support President Truman in his decision to fire MacArthur.

relieved MacArthur of his duty.

While he likely felt disappointed by the way things turned out, MacArthur probably wasn't surprised he was fired, and he never complained about it. After reading the letter the president sent informing him of his decision, MacArthur accepted his dismissal and turned to his wife. "Jeannie," he said, "we're going home at last." ✑

10 AN AMERICAN HERO

Chapter

❧❧❧❧

Upon his return to the United States, MacArthur was welcomed home as a hero. He'd left Japan a hero as well. About 250,000 people had lined the streets to wish him a fond farewell. Many of those watching him leave showed faces streaked with tears.

Back in the United States, the MacArthur family took up residence in New York City in the luxurious Waldorf Towers. Out of respect for MacArthur, the owner of the Waldorf Towers enlarged a space for the war hero and charged him a very modest rent— much less than the space was worth.

In retirement, MacArthur filled his time going to sporting events. He loved boxing, baseball, and, of course, football. He also enjoyed the escape of big Broadway musicals. Other than these entertaining

General MacArthur's car approaches Times Square during his hero's welcome in New York City.

General Douglas MacArthur at age 80

outings, he spent much of his free time at home with his wife and son.

But he wasn't ready to stop working completely. He believed that staying busy and productive was the key to living a happy, healthy life. He served as the Sperry Rand Corporation's chairman of the board and traveled to the office—about an hour from New York City—three or four times a week. He offered advice on international affairs and brought the company recognition just by his presence.

The people in Japan didn't forget MacArthur either. On June 21, 1960, they honored him with the country's highest award available to foreigners who weren't leaders of countries. "No honor I have ever received moves me more deeply," MacArthur said. "Perhaps this is because I can recall no parallel in history where a great nation recently at war has so distinguished its former enemy commander."

Other honors followed, including the cherished Sylvanus Thayer Medal, the highest honor bestowed by West Point. In accepting the award, MacArthur spoke to the young cadets about the soldiers with whom he'd served and his love for West Point. He also told the cadets to live honorable lives:

> *Duty-Honor-Country. Those three ... words reverently dictate what you ought to be, what you can be, what you will be. They are your rallying points; to build courage when courage seems to fail; to regain faith when there seems to be little cause for faith; to create hope when hope becomes forlorn. This does not mean that you are war mongers. On the contrary, the soldier ... prays for peace, for he must suffer and bear the deepest wounds and scars of war.*

MacArthur's life fascinated the public. For years, movie producers and book publishers tried to talk MacArthur into telling his story. Finally, toward the

A painting of MacArthur's Sylvanus Thayer Medal acceptance speech honors the general as well as all U.S. soldiers who have served their country.

end of his life, he did. He knew the resulting money would provide financial security for his wife and son.

While MacArthur lived long enough to finish his story, he'd never held the actual book in his hands. Throughout his life, he hated going to the doctor. As a soldier, he put up with doctors' exams because he felt it was his duty as a military man to keep his body in top physical condition. After his retirement, however, he avoided medical care.

But in early 1964, MacArthur couldn't ignore how sick he was. An Army doctor finally convinced the 84-year-old to submit to surgery to find out why he was ill. MacArthur flew from his home in New York to Walter Reed Medical Center in Washington, D.C.

On March 6, he underwent surgery to remove his gallbladder and gallstones. He seemed to be recovering well, until other problems arose a week later. On April 3 he slipped into a coma, and on April 5 he died with his wife and son at his side.

Americans mourned MacArthur's death. He lived up to West Point's motto—duty, honor, country. No other military officer in American history has equaled his achievements during his 50 years of service. Although not a flawless general, he was an outstanding leader. In MacArthur's honor, President Lyndon Johnson ordered that flags be flown at half-staff until after the funeral. Johnson also called for 19-gun salutes at all American military posts around the world.

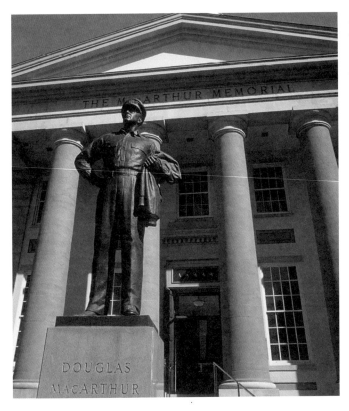

A statue of the general stands at the entry to the MacArthur Memorial.

Douglas MacArthur was buried in Norfolk, Virginia, the city where his mother had been born. The community offered a square city block for his final resting place. In addition, a museum was built to stand as a tribute to him. Always one to enjoy glory, MacArthur had arranged for his memory to live on through this memorial. Although not as grand as a presidential library, the MacArthur Memorial sustains the general's memory and shares the history of the time he lived in with the generations to come.

MacArthur's Life

1903

Graduates from West
Point and is sent to
the Philippines as
an engineer

1880

Born on January 26 in
Little Rock, Arkansas

1905

Serves as an aide to
his father in Japan

1900

1881

The first Japanese
political parties
are formed

1903

Brothers Orville
and Wilbur Wright
successfully fly a
powered airplane

World Events

1913

Serves on the General Staff in Washington, D.C.

1917

Heads to France to help fight the Germans during World War I

1919

Begins his job as superintendent of West Point

1915

1913

Henry Ford begins to use standard assembly lines to produce automobiles

1917

Vladimir Lenin and Leon Trotsky lead Bolsheviks in a rebellion against the czars in Russia during the October Revolution

1919

World War I peace conference begins at Versailles, France

MacArthur's Life

1922

Marries his first wife, Henriette Louise Cromwell Brooks, on February 14; is sent back to the Philippines

1929

Is divorced from Louise

1935

Goes back to the Philippines to serve as a military adviser; his mother dies

1935

1926

Claude Monet and Mary Cassat, well-known impressionist painters, die

1933

Nazi leader Adolf Hitler is named chancellor of Germany

1920

American women get the right to vote

World Events

1938

Son, Arthur IV, is
born on February 21

1937

Marries Jean Marie
Faircloth on April 30
in New York City

1941

Named commander of
the U.S. Army in the
Far East

1940

1939

German troops invade
Poland; Britain and
France declare war
on Germany; World
War II (1939–1945)
begins

MacArthur's Life

1942

Sent from the
Philippines to
Australia; named
Father of the Year

1944

In July, meets with
President Roosevelt
at Pearl Harbor; in
October, returns to
the Philippines and
begins the march to
liberate the islands

1945

Accepts the Japanese
surrender aboard the
USS *Missouri*

1945

The United Nations
is founded

World Events

1950

Leads successful landing at Inchon, Korea

1951

Leaves Japan and returns to the United States after being relieved of his command in Korea

1964

Undergoes surgery in March; dies April 5 at Walter Reed Hospital in Washington, D.C.; buried in Norfolk, Virginia, on April 11

1950

1953

The first Europeans climb Mount Everest

1963

Dr. Martin Luther King Jr. delivers his "I Have a Dream" speech to more than 250,000 people attending the March on Washington

DATE OF BIRTH: January 26, 1880

BIRTHPLACE: Arsenal Barracks of Little Rock, Arkansas

FATHER: Arthur MacArthur Jr. (1845-1912)

MOTHER: Mary Pinkney MacArthur (1852-1935)

EDUCATION: Graduate of United States Military Academy at West Point

FIRST SPOUSE: Henriette Louise Cromwell Brooks (c. 1885-?)

DATE OF MARRIAGE: 1922

SECOND SPOUSE: Jean Marie Faircloth (1899-2000)

DATE OF MARRIAGE: 1937

CHILDREN: Arthur MacArthur IV (1938–)

DATE OF DEATH: April 5, 1964

PLACE OF BURIAL: Norfolk, Virginia

In the Library

Ambrose, Stephen E. *The Good Fight: How World War II Was Won.* New York: Atheneum Books for Young Readers, 2001.

Finkelstein, Norman H. *The Empire General: A Biography of Douglas MacArthur.* Minneapolis: Dillon Press, 1989.

Fox, Mary Virginia. *The Importance of Douglas MacArthur.* San Diego: Lucent Books, 1999.

Gaines, Ann Graham. *Douglas MacArthur: Brilliant General, Controversial Leader.* Berkeley Heights, N.J.: Enslow, 2001.

Scott, Robert Alan. *Douglas MacArthur and the Century of War.* New York: Facts on File, 1997.

Look for more Signature Lives
books about this era:

Andrew Carnegie: *Captain of Industry*

Carrie Chapman Catt: *A Voice for Women*

Henry B. Gonzalez: *Congressman of the People*

J. Edgar Hoover: *Controversial FBI Director*

Langston Hughes: *The Voice of Harlem*

Eleanor Roosevelt: *First Lady of the World*

Elizabeth Cady Stanton: *Social Reformer*

Additional Resources

On the Web

For more information on *Douglas MacArthur*, use FactHound to track down Web sites related to this book.

1. Go to *www.facthound.com*
2. Type in a search word related to this book or this book ID: 0756509947
3. Click on the *Fetch It* button.

FactHound will fetch the best Web sites for you.

Historic Sites

The MacArthur Memorial
MacArthur Square
Norfolk, VA 23510
757/441-2965
To visit the burial site of Douglas and Jean MacArthur, which features a museum dedicated to the general's life and the time in which he lived

MacArthur Museum of Arkansas Military History
503 E. Ninth St.
Little Rock, AR 72202
501/376-4602
To view the site of Douglas MacArthur's birth; the museum preserves the contributions of Arkansas men and women who served in the armed forces

aggressors
countries that attack others without a good
reason

carnage
massive slaughter in war

commonwealth
a state or nation that rules itself but also
maintains ties to a larger nation

communists
people who believe in a social system in which
goods and property are shared in common

economy
the way a country runs its industry, trade,
or finance

guerrilla
a soldier who is not part of a country's
regular army

incomprehensible
unable to be understood

infantry
soldiers who fight on foot

lousy
covered with lice

peremptory
putting an end to all arguements or actions

riding crop
a short whip

unequivocal
clear and without any doubt

Chapter 1

Page 10, line 26: *Douglas MacArthur. Courage Was the Rule: General Douglas MacArthur's Own Story.* New York: McGraw-Hill Book Company, 1965, p. 41.

Page 11, line 6: Ibid, p. 41.

Chapter 2

Page 17, line 7: Ibid., p. 21.

Page 18, line 17: Ibid., p. 23.

Page 19, line 3: Alfred Steinberg. *Douglas MacArthur.* New York: G.P. Putnam's Sons, 1961, p. 14.

Page 21, line 7: *Courage Was the Rule: General Douglas MacArthur's Own Story,* p. 25.

Page 23, line 4: Ibid., p. 30.

Page 23, line 11: Ibid., p. 30.

Page 24, line 1: Ibid., p. 31.

Chapter 3

Page 28, line 4: *Douglas MacArthur,* p. 26.

Page 30, line 12: *Courage Was the Rule: General Douglas MacArthur's Own Story,* p. 46.

Page 31, line 1: Ibid., p. 46.

Page 31, line 21: Ibid., pp. 48–49.

Page 32, line 10: Ibid., p. 49.

Page 33, line 6: Ibid., p. 52.

Chapter 4

Page 35, line 12: Ibid., p. 53.

Page 39, line 26: Ibid., p. 64.

Page 40, line 6: Ibid., p. 65.

Page 41, line 26: Ibid., p. 66.

Page 42, line 21: Ibid., p. 68.

Page 43, line 11: Ibid., p. 69.

Chapter 5

Page 47, line 4: Geoffrey Perret. *Old Soldiers Never Die: The Life of Douglas MacArthur.* New York: Random House, 1996, p. 114.

Page 49, line 2: William Manchester. *American Caesar: Douglas MacArthur 1880-1964.* Boston: Little, Brown and Company, 1978, p. 129.

Page 51, line 12: *Courage Was the Rule: General Douglas MacArthur's Own Story,* p. 105.

Page 52, line 26: Ibid., p. 114.

Chapter 6

Page 56, line 20: Ibid., p. 120.

Page 60, line 5: Ibid., p. 130.

Page 61, line 20: Ibid., p. 139.

Page 63, line 1: Ibid., pp. 146.

Chapter 7

Page 66, line 17: *Old Soldiers Never Die: The Life of Douglas MacArthur*, p. 345.

Page 71, line 1: Ibid., p. 406.

Page 71, line 10: Ibid., p. 407.

Chapter 8

Page 73, line 12: *MacArthur*, p. 133.

Page 74, line 6: Ibid., p. 133.

Page 75, line 3: *Douglas MacArthur*, p. 137.

Page 75, line 11: *Old Soldiers Never Die: The Life of Douglas MacArthur*, p. 447.

Page 75, line 12: Ibid., p. 447.

Page 78, line 10: *Douglas MacArthur*, p. 144.

Page 78, line 18: *MacArthur*, p. 154.

Page 79, line 4: *American Caesar: Douglas MacArthur 1880-1964*, p. 465.

Page 79, line 10: Ibid., p. 465.

Page 80, line 1: *Courage Was the Rule: General Douglas MacArthur's Own Story*, p. 203.

Page 81, line 12: Ibid., p. 210.

Chapter 9

Page 88, line 19: *Old Soldiers Never Die: The Life of Douglas MacArthur*, p. 567.

Page 89, line 7: Ibid., p. 568.

Chapter 10

Page 92, line 21: *Douglas MacArthur*, p. 184.

Page 93, line 4: *Courage Was the Rule: General Douglas MacArthur's Own Story*, p. 280-284.

MacArthur, Douglas. *Courage Was the Rule: General Douglas MacArthur's Own Story.* New York: McGraw-Hill Book Company, 1965.

Manchester, William. *American Caesar: Douglas MacArthur 1880-1964.* Boston: Little, Brown and Company, 1978.

Mayer, Sydney L. *MacArthur.* New York: Ballantine Books Inc., 1971.

PBS American Experience Web site, http://www.pbs.org/wgbh/amex/macarthur/.

Perret, Geoffrey. *Old Soldiers Never Die: The Life of Douglas MacArthur.* New York: Random House, 1996.

Steinberg, Alfred. *Douglas MacArthur.* New York: G.P. Putnam's Sons, 1961.

Brenda Haugen started in the newspaper business and had a career as an award-winning journalist before finding her niche as an author. Since then, she has written and edited many books, most of them for children. A graduate of the University of North Dakota in Grand Forks, Brenda lives in North Dakota with her family.

Image Credits